FALLING IN TIME

FALLING IN TIME

C.E. GATCHALIAN

Falling In Time
first published 2012 by
Scirocco Drama
An imprint of J. Gordon Shillingford Publishing Inc.

Scirocco Drama Editor: Glenda MacFarlane
Cover design by Terry Gallagher/Doowah Design Inc.
Author photo and production photos by Michael O'Shea
Printed and bound in Canada on 100% post-consumer recycled paper.

We acknowledge the financial support of the Manitoba Arts Council and The Canada Council for the Arts for our publishing program.

Excerpts from *Falling In Time* have appeared, in somewhat different form, in the literary magazine *ricepaper* and the anthology *Refractions: Solo* (Playwrights Canada Press). The excerpt from "The Sea and the Butterfly" is by Kim Kirim and translated by Kim Jahhuin in *Contemporary Korean Poetry* (Mosaic Press, www.mosaic-ress.com, 1994). All rights reserved. Reprinted by permission of the publisher.

Production inquiries should be addressed to:
Charles Northcote, Core Literary Inc.
140 Wolfrey Avenue
Toronto, ON M4K 1L3
416-466-4929
charlesnorthcote@rogers.com

Library and Archives Canada Cataloguing in Publication

Gatchalian, C. E., 1974-
Falling in time/C.E. Gatchalian.

A play.
ISBN 978-1-897289-73-0

I. Title.

PS8613.A875F35 2012 C812'.6 C2012-901275-0

J. Gordon Shillingford Publishing
P.O. Box 86, RPO Corydon Avenue, Winnipeg, MB Canada R3M 3S3

For Seán Cummings, for everything.

Acknowledgments

To the Canada Council for the Arts, the BC Arts Council, the City of Vancouver, Origins Theatre Projects and the family of Gordon Armstrong for financially assisting me in the writing of this play; to Dafna Zur and Jenny Ye Kyung Sung for the Korean translations; to my primary dramaturges, Nigel Shawn Williams, Martin Kinch, and Seán Cummings for their rigour and bottomless insight; to Nina Lee Aquino, Greg MacArthur, Stephane Kirkland, Adrienne Wong, Amanda Lockitch and my agent, Charlie Northcote, for additional invaluable dramaturgical feedback; and to my students at ESL Choices, Class of 2004, for enlightening, inspiring and touching me.

Characters

Main:

STEVE:	65 (in some scenes he's in his early 20s). Rugged and handsome. Looks younger than his age. Played by a male actor.
JAMIE:	30. Preppy young ESL teacher, intellectual, aloof. Played by a male actor.
CHANG HYUN:	22. Good-looking young Korean, fresh from military service. Played by a male actor.
EUN HA:	65. Korean woman, Chang Hyun's grandmother. Played by a female actor.
TYRONE:	early 20s. Korean soldier during the Korean War. Played by the actor who plays Chang Hyun.

Subsidiary:

JIN HEE, DOCTOR, MAN #1, MAN #2, COLONEL BARTLETT, BILLIE HOLIDAY, BRENDA, CHINESE SOLDIER, NORTH KOREAN SOLDIER, OLD WOMAN

Voices:

50s radio reporter, voices of Korean soldiers, 50's radio boxing commentator

***

A slash (/) indicates the point of interruption in overlapping dialogue.

Production History

The world premiere of *Falling In Time* was produced by Screaming Weenie Productions, in association with the Vancouver Playhouse and Meta.for Theatre, at Performance Works in Vancouver. It opened on November 5, 2011, with the following cast:

EUN HA .... Manami Hara

CHANG HYUN .... Nelson Wong

JAMIE..Kevin Kraussler

STEVE .... Allan Morgan

Directed by Seán Cummings

Set and Lighting Design by Itai Erdal

Sound Design by Michael Rinaldi

Costume and Prop Design by Christopher David Gauthier

Stage Management by Jethelo E. Cabilete

Technical Direction by Tim Furness

Production Management by Dani Fecko and Kenji Maeda

Set and Lighting Assistance by Mandi Lau

Production Research and Cultural Consultation by Jenny Ye Kyung Sung

The play's development partner was PTC (Vancouver). It also received workshops at the Firehall Arts Centre's BC Buds Spring Arts Fair (Vancouver) in 2006 and 2007, and at Factory Theatre's CrossCurrents Festival (Toronto) in 2007.

Note on Physical Transformations

Onstage physical transformations from one character to another can be and should be done quickly and efficiently—for example, the transformations of the characters into Billie Holiday can be achieved simply by placing a gardenia above the ear.

The transformations of the actor who plays Eun Ha from female to male can, for the most part, be done by use of male clothing (i.e. ties, pants, hats).

Note on the Singing of the Billie Holiday Songs

The actors are to sing the Billie Holiday songs, not lip-sync them. The main idea behind the men transforming into Billie Holiday is not that they're transforming into Billie Holiday, but that they're crossing over into the feminine. The songs are to be sung sincerely, not campily.

(l to r): Allan Morgan (Steve) and Nelson Wong (Chang Hyun).

C.E. Gatchalian

Filipino-Canadian author C.E. Gatchalian was born, raised and is based in Vancouver. He writes plays, poetry, fiction and essays. An alumnus of the University of British Columbia's Creative Writing program, he is the author of nine plays, including *Motifs & Repetitions, Crossing, Broken* and *People Like Vince*. A finalist for the 2003 Lambda Literary Award and the winner of the 2005 Gordon Armstrong Playwright's Rent Award, he has been Playwright-in-Residence at the Playhouse Theatre Company and the Firehall Arts Centre in Vancouver, and Writer-in-Residence at the Berton House Writers' Retreat in Dawson City, Yukon. His work has appeared on stages in Vancouver, Winnipeg, Toronto and New Zealand. Since December 2011 he has been Artistic Producer of Screaming Weenie Productions. Website: www.cegatchalian.com.

Pre-show: The lights dim slightly and we hear Billie Holiday singing "Ghost of Yesterday." As the song progresses the lights gradually dim to black.

Prelude

Lights up on EUN HA, seated, frail and ailing, facing the audience. She rises, looks intently at the audience, addresses them.

		English translation.
EUN HA:	Na jjom bua.	Look at me.
	Pause.	
	Iro sot.	Stand up.
	Pause.	
	Mori lul manjo.	Touch your hair.
	She touches her hair.	
	Olgul.	Your face.
	She touches her face.	
	Bal.	Your arms.
	She touches her arms.	
	Tari.	Your legs.
	She touches her legs.	

Tesso.	There now.
Pause.	
Ta wasso.	You are here.
Light dims.	

Act I

Scene One

Lights up. Vancouver, 1994. School. CHANG HYUN and JAMIE are seated in their respective chairs.

JAMIE: So.

Chang Hyun.

Who's your best friend?

CHANG HYUN: My best-uh priend-uh.

JAMIE: Best. Friend.

CHANG HYUN: Best-uh. Priend-uh.

JAMIE: Best.

CHANG HYUN: Best-uh.

JAMIE: Friend.

CHANG HYUN: Priend-uh.

JAMIE: Not "best-uh." Best. Not "priend-uh." Friend. F, fuh, friend.

CHANG HYUN: Best-uh. Priend-uh.

JAMIE: OK. So who's your best friend?

CHANG HYUN: My best-uh priend-uh.

Pause.

My grandmahduh.

Pause.

JAMIE: Grandmother. Mother. Thuhs and duhs. Thuhs and duhs.

CHANG HYUN: Grandmahduh. Grandmahduh.

JAMIE: So your best friend's your grandmother? Could you elaborate on that?

CHANG HYUN: Pardon?

JAMIE: Could you elaborate on that?

CHANG HYUN: Elaborate.

JAMIE: Elaborate. Verb. To explain something in detail.

CHANG HYUN: Why you use hard word?

JAMIE: Why *do* you use hard words.

CHANG HYUN: Why you use hard word?

JAMIE: Why do I use hard words? Because it would make no sense for me to talk down to you. You're here to improve your English, so you need to rise to my level. So. Your best friend's your grandmother?

CHANG HYUN: Yeah-yeah.

Pause.

JAMIE: Could you elaborate on that?

CHANG HYUN: Elaborate.

JAMIE: Elaborate. Verb. To explain something in detail.

Pause.

CHANG HYUN: Where dat word comes prom?

JAMIE: Pardon?

CHANG HYUN: Where dat word comes prom?

JAMIE: Where *does* that word *come* from. You need does between where and that. It's come, not comes. From, not prom. That, not dat. P's and F's. Thuhs and duhs.

Silence.

CHANG HYUN: Where dat word comes prom?

JAMIE: This is a conversation class, not an etymology one.

CHANG HYUN: Etymo…

JAMIE: Etymology. Noun. The origin of words.

CHANG HYUN: Origi…

JAMIE: Origin. Noun. The point at which something begins.

Silence.

CHANG HYUN: Where dat word comes prom?

Pause.

JAMIE: As I said, this is a conversation class, not an etymology one. I'm not mandated to explain to you the origin of individual words. However, since you asked, elaborate derives from the Latin, *elaborare*: to work out, acquire by labour. Elaborate. Elaborate. So. Your best friend's your grandmother?

Silence.

Would you care to tell me about her?

Pause.

CHANG HYUN: Care to…

JAMIE: Care to means like to. Would you care to tell me about her?

Silence.

At this point EUN HA, with deliberate, ritualistic movements, begins to physically morph into the DOCTOR.

CHANG HYUN: My grandmahduh. Yeah-yeah. She gib bird (birth) to my pahduh. My pahduh he is bud (bird). Beautipul, Beautipul bud. Den he meets mahduh. My mahduh she is bear. Big bird meet bear. Paektu-san bolcano. Dey marry, hab son. I grow, discober Pyongyang, Nord Korea, you know? I Great Leader. Ep, puh, priend. Fees and Eps. Thuhs and duhs.

Silence.

JAMIE: So, your pahduh—I mean, your father, he—

Lights down.

Scene Two

Lights up. A doctor's office. STEVE is seated.

Enter DOCTOR, file in hand. The expression on his face is exceedingly cold. He is looking down at his file.

DOCTOR: Mr. Wendland, the results are back. It's cancer and you are in Stage Four. Any questions?

Silence.

STEVE: You're nuts.

Beat.

You're fucking nuts.

Steely.

There's nothing wrong with me. I'm fine. Do you hear me? I'm fine.

Beat.

Now it's your turn, mister. Tell me I'm fine.

DOCTOR: Mr. Wendland—

STEVE: Just say it, you wuss: I'm fine!

Pause.

DOCTOR: Mr. Wendland, you're not fine. / You're—

STEVE: *(Violently grabbing him by the collar.)* I'm fine! I'm fucking fine! Fucking say it or…

Pause. The DOCTOR says nothing, remains very cold. STEVE lets him go, chuckles.

Why should I listen to some four-eyed ninny who can't even look me straight in the eye?

He grabs his coat.

I refuse to whittle away. I refuse to not exist. I refuse to be a lab mouse for geeks in white suits who think they're destined to inherit the earth.

Beat.

I'm fine. I'm perfectly fine. I'm outta here.

Beat.

I've always been able to figure things out on my own, buddy, and I've been right one hundred percent of the time. So here's what I've got figured out about this thing you say I have: it's nothing that a simple life adjustment can't cure.

Beat.

And what, pray tell, would that life adjustment be? Doing a few more reps in the gym, eating a few more veggies for supper, and keeping the hell away from people like you who are trying to bring me down.

Beat. Talking into the DOCTOR's face.

No one's bringing me down, Doc. I'll see you at your grave.

He exits. Fade out.

Scene Three

Lights up on CHANG HYUN and JAMIE. School. The DOCTOR begins to morph back into EUN HA.

JAMIE: So, Chang Hyun, what do you like better, cats or dogs?

Silence.

Chang Hyun?

Pause.

CHANG HYUN: Actually, I don't like animal.

JAMIE: Animals.

CHANG HYUN: Animal. I hate dem. But ip I hab to choose—

JAMIE: If. F.

CHANG HYUN: Ip I hab to choose, I choose dog.

JAMIE: Tense. Conditional.

CHANG HYUN: I choose dog, because dey make good meal.

JAMIE: Good meal? Article?

CHANG HYUN: Good meal. Belly (very) delicious.

JAMIE: V. Vuh. Very.

CHANG HYUN: B. Buh. Belly. Delicious.

JAMIE: You've eaten dog?

CHANG HYUN: Isn't it "a dog"?

JAMIE: No, because we're using dog as food.

CHANG HYUN: So?

JAMIE: When you talk about animals as food they're not countable. You don't say, "I ate a fish." You don't say, "I ate a chicken."

CHANG HYUN: But you say, "I ate an apple."

JAMIE: That's different.

CHANG HYUN: Why?

JAMIE: Because apples aren't animals.

Pause.

CHANG HYUN: Why?

JAMIE: Why what?

CHANG HYUN: Why all dese rule?

JAMIE: Rules.

CHANG HYUN: Rule.

JAMIE: Every language has rules.

CHANG HYUN: I mean, why article bepore pruit and no article bepore animal?

JAMIE: I don't know.

CHANG HYUN: You don't?

JAMIE: All languages are arbitrary, self-enclosed systems, the rules of which must be learned by practice and by rote. There is no logical, intrinsic reason for anything.

Pause.

So. You've eaten dog?

Silence.

Chang Hyun?

Silence.

Chang Hyun?

CHANG HYUN: Ip dere no…logical, intrinsic…reason por anysing den I just go.

CHANG HYUN exits. Fade out.

Scene Four

Sound FX: Bar. People talking and laughing, glasses clinking, etc.

STEVE: I tell ya… *(Lights up on STEVE in a bar, on a stool, drink in hand, inebriated, talking to some unseen other.)* the Canucks have gotta fucking brush up on their defense. Did you see that game against the Rangers? Fucking incompetence. 3-2, five minutes left in the third. A fucking one goal lead they had and the Rangers quiet as pansies. Then some fifth-line teeny bopper from a farm team ends up tying it. How in hell on God's green earth did that fucking happen? I'll tell you how: they fucking fell asleep. They may as well have emptied the ice and the net coz the path was fucking clear for them to score that goal. Jesus, they fell asleep. But they're playing for a sleepy-ass city—how can they not fall asleep? Even my hometown in Indiana had more get-up than this lotus-roost. You know what happens when people fall asleep, buddy boy? They die. They fucking die. I for one never sleep. OK, I nod off a coupla hours or so but I don't sleep the way others do, and you know why? Coz sleep's for sissies. It's—

Lights snap out, 1-count. Lights up. Again he is talking to some unseen other.

Kimchi, you know what kimchi is, don't you? You don't? What, you just crawl out of the backwoods? You've never heard of kimchi? Where you from? Surrey? Kimchi, Christ, it's only the best food ever created. It gets you revved up, it gets you all horny—I fucked like a rabbit when I was back in Korea. A lot of Korean bitches had a fill of this here *(Points to his crotch.)* and are happier women for it. You think in a million years they'd get what I gave them from their men? They're a bit…under-blessed, to put it, as they say, delicately. But kimchi, fuck, it made a warrior out of me. I'd sneak as much as I could into the barracks and I'd eat it every morning, I'd get this fucking rush and my day'd be all set. I got into amazing shape—my biceps were hard as melons *(Flexes his biceps.)*—still got them, by the way, not bad for a pensioner. But more important I was a great soldier, so great that after the war I decided to keep doin' it, coz it was my vocation, my calling, like some are called to the priesthood. Did I tell ya that during the war I got by on a measly two hours of sleep every day? When everyone else was asleep I was busy doing push-ups. Coz you know what happens when people sleep, don't ya? They die, they fucking die.

Lights snap out, 1-count. Lights up. Again he is talking to some unseen other.

Boxers today—they got nothing on Marciano. Saw him fight his last fight. Live in Yankee Stadium, two years after Korea. Caught a hop there from

Fort Riley. The most beautiful moment of my life. A fucking gladiator he was. Bullet-like passes, both hands, both hands. Then he'd work his way in and wham-BAM the uppercut, Moore's head snapping back like a petal off a daisy. Now he floored Rocky in the second but Rocky came storming back, he wasn't about to let his perfect record slip away. He knocked the sucker down five, count 'em, five times. *(Throwing punches in the air.)* Right, left, right right, DOWN. Left, right right, left, DOWN, DOWN, DOWN, DOWN! *(He yelps with glee.)* 49 and 0. Perfection attained. Blood, vomit, and yellow-skinned commies. But at home, in that ring, there was God.

Lights snap out, 1-count. Lights up. Again he is talking to some unseen other.

Jazz. You like jazz? What d'ya mean, you hate it? More like you don't understand it. You can't hate what you don't understand now, can you? There's no shame in admitting you're stupid. In fact more people should—the world would run a hell of a lot smoother if they did. If you, for example, would just admit you're stupid, you wouldn't be here arguing with me now and we'd both be having a nicer time. I heard 'em all, live…Charlie Parker, Miles Davis, John Coltrane, Lester Young. Saw Billie Holiday in a club in Cincy. A year from the grave and looking like a pile of bamboo sticks, long gloves to cover the needle marks, high as a fucking kite. But it didn't matter—she was singing, singing in that special way of hers, like she didn't fucking care, except you knew she cared too much. I swear if teardrops had a voice, they'd sound like Billie Holiday. The lifeline, I called it—that's what her voice was, this line from the soul that carried all of life's wears and tears. The last song she sang that night was "T'ain't Nobody's Business If I Do." Chin up, brow arched, it was like she was saying, "Ain't gonna change, ain't following no law but my own. Gonna keep going, ain't never giving up."

Lights snap out.

Scene Five

Lights up on CHANG HYUN and JAMIE. School.

JAMIE: Chang Hyun.

Beat.

Glad you're back.

Beat.

CHANG HYUN: I already pay dis lesson, so it's waste obu (of) my pahduh's money ip I don't come.

JAMIE: Tense. Past conditional.

Pause, as though expecting a response.

It would have been a waste of money. And mood. Subjunctive.

Pause, as though expecting a response.

If I didn't come. And it's if. F. Fuh.

CHANG HYUN: I speak English da way I want. Sank (thank) you.

Silence.

JAMIE: OK. Where did we leave off yesterday?

Pause.

Oh yes, I remember. You told me you've eaten dog.

Beat.

Tell me about eating dog.

Pause.

CHANG HYUN: No.

JAMIE: Why not?

CHANG HYUN: Because you just want make pun obu Korea.

JAMIE: That's not true. I honestly am very curious about what dog tastes like.

CHANG HYUN: You just want to peel superior to Korea. You Westerner always sink (think) you're superior.

JAMIE: That may be true of some Westerners, but if you knew anything about me you'd know that I don't think that at all.

CHANG HYUN: What you sink den?

JAMIE: I ask the questions here. What does dog taste like?

Beat.

CHANG HYUN: Belly (bery) delicious. Belly juicy. Taste like chicken but better. More tender.

JAMIE: Very delicious. Very, not belly.

CHANG HYUN: We eat it in hot wedder (weather), it make us more cool.

JAMIE: Superior of cool. Cool./Er.

CHANG HYUN: In Korea in old day we hab no cattle.

JAMIE: The old days. And tense./Tense.

CHANG HYUN: We need protein, so we eat dogs.

JAMIE: Dog as food is singular/not plural.

CHANG HYUN: But dog we eat is not same as pet.

JAMIE: You've forgotten your/articles.

CHANG HYUN: We raise separately, pet dogs prom pood dogs.

JAMIE: P's and F's. P's/and F's

CHANG HYUN: You sink we sabage-ee, but we not sabage-ee.

JAMIE: V./Vuh. Savage. Savage.

CHANG HYUN: In some country dey eat horses. In/Korea dat's disgusting.

JAMIE: Animals as food./Singular, not plural.

CHANG HYUN: In Puransu (France) dey eat snail. Why you not/ sink dat's disgusting?

JAMIE: Animals as food./Singular, not plural.

CHANG HYUN: But dog is like...aprodisiac... it make us puck all/ da time, dree, pour time a day.

At this point EUN HA, with deliberate, ritualistic movements, begins to physically morph into MAN #1.

JAMIE: Aphrodisiac. Phuh.

CHANG HYUN: Aprodisiac. Puh.

JAMIE: Fuck. Fuck.

CHANG HYUN: Puck. Puck.

JAMIE: *(Rising from chair.)* Fuck. Fuck.

CHANG HYUN: Na ri na ri kae na ri

Ip beh tta ta mul/ko yo

JAMIE: ENGLISH/ONLY.

CHANG HYUN: Kip un san sok ong tal sam

Nu ka wa so/mok na yo

JAMIE: ENGLISH ONLY! I'M THE TEACHER HERE AND YOU'RE JUST A FUCKING STUDENT. *(Controlling himself, under his breath, more to himself.)* I have a Master's degree for Christ's sake and I own a fucking bike. I've worked my ass off to get here so this room is mine.

Silence.

CHANG HYUN: *(Unfazed.)* We only eat dogs on special—

Lights down.

Scene Six

Light on STEVE and MAN #1, the latter giving the former a blow job. STEVE's apartment.

STEVE: *(Mumbling breathlessly.)* Faster. Faster. Didn't I tell you I want it fast? Kids today, you've got nothing on us. Coz we fucking had to work. We fucking had to endure. Any idea what war's like? Vomit. Blood. Yellow-skinned commies. You're not following, are you, you—

Lights down, 1-count.

Lights up. STEVE is fucking MAN #1 standing up, from behind.

Any idea what that's like? Of course not, coz you're spoiled...selfish...young guys today, you're all spoiled and selfish...going through fire, that's what makes you a man. What have you had to fight for? Getting a cherry on your sundae? And now you think you're a strapping stud coz you're being plugged by a war vet—

Lights down.

Scene Seven

Lights up on CHANG HYUN and JAMIE. School. MAN #1 begins to morph back into EUN HA.

JAMIE: Chang Hyun.

Pause.

I know you don't like me.

Pause.

And I wouldn't have it any other way.

Pause.

You're not supposed to like me. I'm the teacher, you're the student. A binary opposition from which we must not deviate.

CHANG HYUN: You sink you're better dan me.

JAMIE: It has nothing to do with that. It has nothing to do with anything. It has nothing to do with "facts," or "truth," or "reality." *(On "facts," "truth" and "reality" JAMIE does air quotes.)* All this is, is play. Play and transformation. Parody. Exaggeration. An "up yours" to the PTB.

CHANG HYUN: PTB?

JAMIE: PTB. The powers that be. Teaching is my life. In this setting, in this room, the PTB is me. So. First topic. What's your dream job?

Pause.

Dream. Job. A job you dream of having.

Pause.

CHANG HYUN: I hab no dream job.

JAMIE: Why not?

CHANG HYUN: Because I don't beeree-ba (believe) in dream. Dream is useless. I care only about reality. So I hab no dream job. Just job I hab to do.

JAMIE: And what job is that?

CHANG HYUN: Managing my pahduh's business.

JAMIE: Which is?

CHANG HYUN: Packaging company in Seoul (pronounced So-ul).

JAMIE: Will you like that job?

CHANG HYUN: No, I hate it. But it's my duty, so I lub it. Job I hate, duty I lub. Widout duty we hab nussing (nothing). Eberysing (Everthing) pall apart.

JAMIE: You don't believe in dreams, but you told me before you believe in God.

CHANG HYUN: Because God is real. God is true.

JAMIE: Many people think that God doesn't exist.

CHANG HYUN: Dey wrong. He exist.

JAMIE: How can you be so sure?

CHANG HYUN: Because He look apter my pamily. My grandmahduh...my pahduh, dey...dey supper bery muchee (much). But dey...surbibe. God protect dem. Widout God we are nussing. God is good.

JAMIE: Your family's success was the result of hard work and determination. I don't think God had much to do with it.

CHANG HYUN: What you saying?

JAMIE: Religion has done more harm to the world than good. It's caused countless wars and cost millions their lives.

CHANG HYUN: My grandmahduh teach me dat God's way not our way. We cannot know what He sink. But eberysing dat happen is because obu Him. And bad sing dat happen make us more strong.

Lights down.

Scene Eight

Music: Billie Holiday singing "T'Ain't Nobody's Business If I Do." Lights up, STEVE's apartment.

Sound FX: The phone rings. STEVE rushes to the phone and picks it up.

STEVE: Hello?

Hi.

You do this a lot?

Me? Are you kidding? I ain't ugly, buddy, I ain't hurting in the popularity department. Just a bit bored tonight is all.

So you like my voice? Huh?

All-American testosterone on this end of the line.

Six feet, one-eighty, salt and pepper hair, blue eyes, muscular.

Seventeen-inch arms, forty-two inch chest, hard, bulging nipples, eight-inch cock, you'll fucking love my cock.

He starts stroking his cock.

Army vet here, Bronze Star for Bravery.

Turn you on? Huh? OK, let's roll.

Starts stroking himself faster.

So we're both of us in a concentration camp. I'm a Nazi, you're a Jew. You know you're gonna die, so you're horny for one last, mind-blowing fuck before we roast ya alive. I slip into your quarters in the middle of the night. You're wide awake, you're fucking panting. I drag you into a little corner, you suck me till I'm hard. You get up, bend over. I ease my cock into your ass. You...

Huh?

I'm the top, you're the bottom.

Listen, buddy, I ain't looking for no top.

Either I fuck the living daylights out of you or this phone call's over.

He slams the phone down.

Fruit.

Lights down.

Scene Nine

Lights up on CHANG HYUN and JAMIE. School.

JAMIE: Chang Hyun. What's your favourite movie?

Pause.

CHANG HYUN: *Sound obu Music.*

JAMIE: Why?

CHANG HYUN: Scene in middle obu mobie. Captain sing and play guitar por pirst time. He has beautipul boice. He and Maria look at each usser (other). Dey hab connection. Dey pall in lub, get marry, lib happily eber apter. It is true story, beautipul story. I want to hate dis mobie because it's...typical...American bullshit. Dey sink all you need is music and good cheer and all da world's problem disappear. Disgusting. And dangerous. Dat's why American get away wis eberysing. Dey can lie, dey can kill, dey can interpere. As long as dere's cute children and pretty tune eberysing okey-dokey. But da story in *Sound obu Music* is beautipul and true. It is how lipe should be. It make me cry.

Lights down on CHANG HYUN.

Scene Ten

Lights remain on JAMIE as he rises and enters his apartment. He rolls a joint, lights it, smokes.

Sound FX: Phone ringing. JAMIE picks up the phone.

JAMIE: Hello? Hello, Mother. How are you?

Oh, the usual. Teaching, teaching, teaching.

Mother, I was home just last Christmas.

Mother, I haven't lived there in twelve years. Why on earth would I want to go back now?

You know as well as I do that there's nothing left for me in Kansas. I don't believe in wizards and I think Dorothy is a bitch.

Mother, I don't care that there's a Democrat in the White House. Clinton has proven to be a colossal disappointment. Utterly spineless, like the rest of the liberal establishment. If he was all *that* you'd all be on your honeymoon now with universal healthcare. Instead, the man cowers to the slightest conservative bullying. Mother, pragmatism is the place of recoil for those too cowardly to lead. You do not govern by consensus if who you're governing is a pack of bumpkins, brainwashed by two centuries of libertarian groupthink. You've got to push them out of the cave and up to the light, even if it kills them. And frankly I hope it does kill them, some of them at least—America could use a few fewer Rush Limbaughs, don't you think? Meanwhile, there are genocides happening in Rwanda and Bosnia that, with no material interests to protect, we've simply watched from the sidelines. So no, Mother, nothing's changed, in fact it's getting worse—with the rise of the fundamentalists we're going the way of the Third Reich. Besides, I'm happy in Vancouver—well, maybe happy is the wrong word, given my propensity for melancholia. But I do feel…inconspicuous here. I don't—stand out here the way I do in Topeka. I suppose I'm loopy everywhere but I'm—closer to the centre in Vancouver. Liberal isn't a dirty word here. And people don't…judge.

I can assure you, Mother, I'm not smoking anything. You know I can't stand that stuff.

He takes a hit.

Lights down.

Scene Eleven

Lights up on CHANG HYUN and JAMIE.

At this point EUN HA, with deliberate, ritualistic movements, begins to morph into MAN #2.

JAMIE: Chang Hyun, what do you think of compulsory military service?

Pause.

Compulsory. Required. As in duty.

Pause.

CHANG HYUN: Nussing.

Pause.

JAMIE: Pardon?

CHANG HYUN: Nussing. I sink nussing.

JAMIE: You served in the military, didn't you? Isn't it compulsory in Korea?

CHANG HYUN: You hab Korean student bepore. You know answer.

JAMIE: But I want to hear what you think.

Pause.

CHANG HYUN: *(Steely.)* Please change-uh topic.

Lights down.

Scene Twelve

This scene contains several mini-scenes that follow each other in a rapid, seamless flow.

Lights up. STEVE's apartment. STEVE and MAN #2 putting their clothes on, post-sex.

MAN #2: My son'd be so ashamed of me right now, not to mention my wife.

Beat.

How 'bout you? You got kids?

Silence.

STEVE: Aesop.

MAN #2: Huh?

STEVE: You know Aesop?

MAN #2: The storyteller?

STEVE: "The Lark Who Buried Her Father." That's a good one. The lark, you know, it was around before the earth was. So anyways the lark, her father dies, right? But the earth isn't around yet, so where does she bury him? In her head. And so she gets her crest, which is really her father's grave.

Pause.

Yeah, I got one. A son.

Lights down on STEVE.

Light up on CHANG HYUN, wearing a muscle shirt, and JAMIE. School.

MAN #2 begins to morph back into EUN HA.

JAMIE: Chang Hyun, let's spice it up and get political. Let's talk about the Korean War.

CHANG HYUN: Why?

JAMIE: It's a subject I'm quite interested in.

CHANG HYUN: Why?

JAMIE: Because it's a war that's hardly ever talked about. The Forgotten War, they call it. And I'm always interested in what's forgotten. Plus my father fought in the war. From what I heard it completely traumatized him.

CHANG HYUN: Your pawduh pought in Korean War?

JAMIE: That's right. I never knew my father. He left us when I was two. And I used to hate Korea because it was there that he lost his marbles. But I've challenged those irrational feelings and am a better person for it.

CHANG HYUN: I don't want to talk about Korean War. Please change-uh topic.

Pause.

JAMIE: Alright, let's talk about the present. Kim Il-sung. He met today with Jimmy Carter. He's agreed to stop his nuclear research program. Carter called it a miracle. He thinks Kim has seen the light. At any rate this may be the beginning of a whole new era for Korea.

Silence.

CHANG HYUN: It will take more dan bisit prom Carter to pix da problem in Korea. And ip u sink Kim has seen light, you are moron.

Please change-uh topic.

Pause.

JAMIE: Fine.

Pause.

Nice shirt.

CHANG HYUN: Sank you.

JAMIE: It makes you look sexy.

CHANG HYUN: Sank you.

Pause.

You remind me obu somebody.

JAMIE: Who?

CHANG HYUN: Maria bon Trapp-uh.

JAMIE: Why?

CHANG HYUN: Bery innocent. Bery nai-buh (naïve). I like.

Lights down.

Lights up on STEVE in a room in the gym. He is performing an exercise.

CHANG HYUN enters humming the Korean folk song "Arirang." He starts performing a biceps exercise. STEVE eyes him.

CHANG HYUN does a set of twelve. STEVE approaches him.

STEVE: If you really wanna work your biceps, there's a better exercise you can do.

CHANG HYUN: Pardon?

STEVE: I said, if you really—

CHANG HYUN: My bicep in good shape.

STEVE: But if you want them in even better shape, there's another exercise you can do.

CHANG HYUN: But my bicep in good shape.

STEVE: But don't you want them in even better shape?

CHANG HYUN: Dey cannot be in better shape because dey are pawpect (perfect).

He flexes his biceps.

STEVE: Your peaks could be better.

CHANG HYUN: Pardon?

STEVE: Your peaks could be better.

CHANG HYUN: Peaks?

STEVE: This here. *(He flexes his biceps.)* See this? *(He points to his bicep.)* This is the peak. See how high mine are?

CHANG HYUN looks at it.

CHANG HYUN: Not dat high.

STEVE: Huh?

CHANG HYUN: Not dat high.

Pause. STEVE grabs a dumbbell and starts performing a curl very slowly—going up slowly, holding the flex position for about six seconds, then going down slowly.

STEVE: *(Doing another rep.)* This is called static contraction. You heard of that?

CHANG HYUN: No.

STEVE: Didn't think so. Static contraction. See how slow I'm doing this rep? And how long I'm holding the flex position? No more than six reps, very slowly.

Once again he holds the flex position for about six seconds. Very intense.

He feigns confidence and assurance during the following speech but he has noticeable physical difficulty performing this exercise (heavy breathing, coughing, etc.).

To stimulate hypertrophy you must expose your muscles to maximum contraction. Hypertrophy happens when the body senses, through neural signals, that it cannot…accommodate the weight presently weighted against…it. Once…the body ascertains…that it must be stronger to complete a particular…exercise… in the future, it spurs…the growth…of additional…muscle.

STEVE is out of breath.

Silence.

CHANG HYUN: Not dat great.

STEVE: Huh?

CHANG HYUN: Your bicep. Not dat great.

Pause.

STEVE: *(Steely-eyed.)* They're great.

CHANG HYUN: Sorry, nod dat great.

Silence.

STEVE inches closer to CHANG HYUN.

STEVE: *(Quietly, menacingly.)* How big's your cock?

CHANG HYUN: Pardon?

STEVE: Your cock.

CHANG HYUN: *(Uncomprehending.)* Your cock?

STEVE: Your dick.

Pause.

CHANG HYUN: I don't know.

STEVE inches closer to CHANG HYUN.

STEVE: Let's find out then. *(Piercing whisper.)* Show me your dick.

CHANG HYUN: Pardon?

STEVE: Your penis. Show me your penis.

CHANG HYUN: What?

STEVE: C'mon, you gook. Pull it out. How the hell else are we gonna measure it?

Pause.

CHANG HYUN: You crazy.

STEVE: *(Exploding.)* YOU HAVE NO RIGHT TO TALK TO ME LIKE THAT! NO FUCKING RIGHT! REMEMBER THIS IS MY COUNTRY! YOU'RE JUST A FUCKING GUEST!

Pause.

So, how big's your cock—oops, I mean penis.

CHANG HYUN: I don't know.

STEVE: Probably a little hamster penis, just like every other gook's.

He reaches out and feels CHANG HYUN's crotch. CHANG HYUN pushes him violently. STEVE falls to the floor. STEVE stands up, smirks, pulls a gun out of his gym bag, points it at CHANG HYUN. CHANG HYUN steps back.

And if you dare call staff I'll fucking kill you.

CHANG HYUN exits, relatively calm. STEVE laughs.

Lights down.

We hear male voices singing an army tune, sung to the melody of "Arirang."

MALE VOICES:

Fly the Stars and Stripes high
For freedom and peace are nigh
Shout for victory and make a pledge that men will be free
Brothers forever
Place your trust in me
Fly the Stars and Stripes high
For peace and freedom are nigh

We then hear the voice of TYRONE singing "Arirang."

VOICE OF TYRONE:

Arirang arirang arariyo
Arirang gokyelo nomokanda
Na lul burigo ga shinun nimun
Shimlido mokgasaw bal byung nanda

Lights up.

Korea, 1950.

STEVE and CHANG HYUN have become, respectively, YOUNG STEVE, a soldier in Korea, and TYRONE.

STEVE: *(Over TYRONE's singing, approaching TYRONE.)* Soldier.

No response.

Soldier.

No response.

Hey.

No response.

Hey!

No response.

O'Brien.

STEVE knocks on TYRONE's helmet.

Could you please look at me when I call you?

TYRONE stops singing, finally looks at him.

TYRONE: We-yo?

STEVE: No "we-yo." English only. When I call you you look at me. Your name is Tyrone. Tyrone O'Brien. OK?

TYRONE: Ye.

STEVE: What's that?

TYRONE: Yeah-yeah. Tyrone. O'Brien.

STEVE: Roll call is at 0500 hours.

TYRONE: Roll call is at 0500 hours.

STEVE: But it's better to be there early.

TYRONE: But it's better to be dere early.

STEVE: Time is of the essence.

TYRONE: Time is obu da essence.

STEVE: Don't repeat everything I say.

TYRONE: Don't repeat eberysing I say.

STEVE: Stop it.

TYRONE: Stop it.

STEVE turns, starts to walk away.

STEVE: *(Under his breath.)* Gook.

TYRONE chuckles, point the rifle at STEVE, the barrel touching his helmet. He knocks on STEVE's helmet with his rifle.

STEVE slowly turns around.

What do you think you're doing?

TYRONE: *(Firmly, but smiling and good natured.)* Cho-e irumun Ju Cheol rago hamnida.

Beat.

My name Ju Cheol. No Tyrone O'Brien. No gook.

He puts his rifle down.

He and STEVE look at each other for a few seconds.

STEVE: Keep it up and I'll have you put on latrine duty.

He exits.

Lights down on TYRONE as he resumes singing "Arirang."

In dimmed lights, we see the actor who plays JAMIE, with deliberate, ritualistic movements, transform himself into JIN HEE, a young Korean woman.

Lights up on CHANG HYUN in his apartment, kneeling by his bed, head bowed, praying.

When he finishes praying, he sits on the bed and opens a letter.

Light up on JIN HEE.

JIN HEE: *(In Korean = perfect English.)*

Chang Hyun,

I am counting the days till you're back home in Seoul—I miss you so much.

I thought waiting for you this time would be easier—when you were away in the military I don't know how I survived. But in a way this time is even worse. You're living in a foreign country speaking a foreign language. Somehow, I can't help but feel that you are becoming a different person, that somehow I'm losing you. You don't call me that much anymore, and you don't return my calls as quickly as you used to. So I can't help but wonder. Then again, you haven't said that anything's wrong, so everything must be OK. But if something is wrong, I want you to be honest with me.

Mind you, if something were to happen to us I think I'd kill myself. But enough of this.

How are your studies coming along? Has your English improved? Are your teachers kind to you?

Anyways, I've started thinking about our wedding and I think we should get married in the country.

As you know my uncle's a pastor, and he's eager to marry us. I've already picked out a dress.

You're not seeing other girls, are you?

Anyways, every day without you is a trial. I love you and miss you.

Jin Hee

After CHANG HYUN finishes reading the letter, he freezes for a few seconds as though reflecting.

He crumples the letter and throws it angrily on the floor as JIN HEE transforms back into JAMIE.

Lights down on CHANG HYUN, dim on JAMIE.

Scene Thirteen

Lights up on CHANG HYUN and JAMIE. School.

JAMIE: Ch—

CHANG HYUN: Jamie. Prom now on don't call me Chang Hyun.

JAMIE: Why not?

CHANG HYUN: Because I hab Western name now.

JAMIE: Have a Western name. B's and V's. B's/and

CHANG HYUN: Call me Windsor.

Pause.

JAMIE: Why Windsor?

CHANG HYUN: Do you know what Windsor means?

JAMIE: No.

CHANG HYUN: I sought (thought) you knew eberysing.

It's Teutonic por "bend in da riber."

Pause.

JAMIE: If selling out is what you choose to do I suppose that's your prerogative. If your raison d'etre is to succumb to Western hegemony / then

CHANG HYUN: Puck you. Just call me Windsor.

Pause.

JAMIE: Alright then. Windsor. What do you think of Vancouver?

CHANG HYUN: It's pretty. Lots obu trees. But bery boring. Nussing to do, so people sink too much. Ask too many question. Become crazy.

JAMIE: Thought is good. Questions are good.

CHANG HYUN: But ip too much you lose direction, porget duty, become lost.

JAMIE: I actually quite like Vancouver. I moved here from Kansas after high school. Kansas was intolerable. Philistine. Obtuse. In Vancouver I was able to start anew.

Scene Fourteen

Lights up on CHANG HYUN and STEVE. They are in a sports pub.

Sound FX: Music, and a myriad of men's and women's voices on top of it.

CHANG HYUN and STEVE are standing about six feet away from each other. CHANG HYUN is smoking. They are both holding drinks. STEVE eyes CHANG HYUN for a while before advancing towards him.

STEVE: Hey.

CHANG HYUN looks at STEVE. He moves to leave but STEVE blocks him.

Look, I'm sorry if I scared you at the gym the other day. I was…having an episode.

CHANG HYUN brushes past him.

Are you Korean?

CHANG HYUN stops, turns back.

CHANG HYUN: How you know I'm Korean?

STEVE: Call it my hidden talent.

CHANG HYUN: Eberyone say Chinese or Japanese.

STEVE: Well I'm not most people. When was the last time someone pointed a gun at you in the gym?

Pause.

I've been to Korea.

CHANG HYUN: Really?

STEVE: Spent time there.

Lights out.

CHANG HYUN: Canadian always sink I am Chinese or Japanese.

STEVE: I'm not Canadian. I'm American.

Beat.

CHANG HYUN: *(Some hostility.)* American?

STEVE: Born and raised. You gotta problem with that?

Pause.

CHANG HYUN: Why you lib in Canada?

STEVE: Just stumbled across the border one weekend and never made it back.

Pause.

CHANG HYUN: People always say Chinese or Japanese, neber Korean.

STEVE: Yeah, people are pretty dense that way.

Pause.

CHANG HYUN: So...you been to Korea?

STEVE: Yup. Fought in the war.

CHANG HYUN: The war. *(Pause.)* Yu kee oh junjeng? (Translation: 6-25—this is how South Koreans refer to the Korean War.)

STEVE: Yup. Yu kee oh junjeng.

Pause.

CHANG HYUN: So…you American?

STEVE: What did I say the first time?

Beat.

CHANG HYUN: Sorry...I don't like American.

STEVE: You don't, eh? OK, I can see what's coming. It was all big bad ugly America's fault.

CHANG HYUN: You promise to make Korea pree and independent nation, but instead you pight. Wis Russia. You make Korea your puppet.

STEVE: We were only doing what we had to do to give your country freedom.

CHANG HYUN: Preedom, what you mean preedom?

STEVE: Freedom to think and believe what you want.

Freedom to make of your life what you want.

CHANG HYUN: You sink people in your inner city habu preedom? America has highest poberty rate in Pirst World.

STEVE: With freedom comes responsibility. Responsibility for your own fate.

CHANG HYUN: Den why don't you let oder country be responsible por deir pate? Why you always interpere?

STEVE: We interfere only when freedom and democracy are under attack. If your northern kinsmen hadn't invaded you the war would never have happened.

CHANG HYUN: You say it is our pault we dibided, but you don't want us to reunite because den you can no longer sell weapon to Sowse (South) Korea.

STEVE: Get your facts straight: Communism didn't work. The whole world's realized that.

CHANG HYUN: America isn't pawpect. You hab many problem.

STEVE: Then go join your northern kinsmen if you love Communism so much.

CHANG HYUN: I'm not Communist, I'm…socialist.

STEVE: Communism with a pretty face. Get off the damn fence.

CHANG HYUN: You know how many Korean die during Korean War? Dey di because obu your stupid war wis Russia. You don't know how much-ee Korea supper.

An enraged look emerges on STEVE's face, but just as he's about to explode the lights snap out, 1-count.

Lights snap back on. STEVE and CHANG HYUN are seated at the bar. The music continues to play.

Windsor. My name's Windsor.

STEVE: That's not your real name.

CHANG HYUN: It's my name in Bancouber.

STEVE: Should give yourself an Irish name.

CHANG HYUN: Why Irish?

STEVE: Coz the Koreans are the Irish of Asia.

CHANG HYUN: Neber heard dat.

STEVE: Hot tempered, disenfranchised, that kinda thing.

Our buddies during the war—we gave them Irish names.

CHANG HYUN: Buddy?

STEVE: The Koreans who volunteered with us. I had a buddy.

Lights change, dim.

In the dimmed lights we see STEVE and CHANG HYUN slinging on rifles to again become STEVE as a young soldier in Korea and TYRONE.

Lights brighten.

Korea, 1950.

TYRONE is singing again. He is holding a white doraji in his hand.

TYRONE: Doraji, doraji, bek doraji
Shimshin / san chuneh bek doraji/
Han dul pooriman /kae-o-do
Dae guangjuri-e ch'ol/ch'ol nomnunda

STEVE: O'Brien.

No response.

O'Brien!

No response.

Tyrone.

No response.

Tyrone!

No response.

STEVE goes to TYRONE and shakes him.

TYRONE: *(Stops singing.)* Ye.

STEVE: Listen up, coz this is the last time I'm gonna tell you this—your name is Tyrone. Tyrone O'Brien. Tyrone. O'Brien.

TYRONE: Cho-e irumun Ju Cheol rago hamnida.

STEVE: English only, soldier. Get your rifle out.

TYRONE: Yeh.

Beat.

STEVE: Target practice. Get your rifle out.

TYRONE doesn't respond. STEVE points to TYRONE's rifle.

This. Here. Get it out.

As TYRONE unslings his rifle the barrel accidentally hits the bottom of STEVE's chin, snapping his head back.

TYRONE: Mianhamnida.

STEVE glares at him. He unslings his rifle and aims it. He is still for a moment then shoots.

STEVE: There. Now do what I did. Aim your rifle there and shoot.

TYRONE aims his rifle. He is still for a moment, then aims the rifle at STEVE and shoots.

TYRONE: *(In Korean.)* Bang!

He produces a flower.

(Reciting from a Korean poem.) Since no one has ever told her
how deep the sea is
the white butterfly has
no fear of the sea.

STEVE: English only.

TYRONE: She lands on the sea taking it
for a batch of blue radish;
she comes home like a princess,
her wings wet in the salt waves.
In the month of March the sea doesn't bloom
and the pale moon chills the thin waist
of the sad butterfly.

Silence.

STEVE: Whatever you think you're trying to pull with these stunts of yours, boy, it ain't gonna work. Just what do you think you're messing with?

STEVE turns.

Lights change, dim. YOUNG STEVE and TYRONE become STEVE and CHANG HYUN again.

Lights brighten.

CHANG HYUN and STEVE are chuckling. They are both quite drunk.

You like to drink, don't you?

CHANG HYUN: Obu cosu (Of course), I am Korean.

STEVE: Like I said, the Irish of Asia.

CHANG HYUN: My girlpriend, she hate it when I drink. She sink I am bad person. One night I drink too much I bomit on her lap. She don't speak to me por one week, so I'm glad I bomit. She neber stop talking. She is bitch.

STEVE: Hey, watch your mouth. Korean women are terrific.

CHANG HYUN: How you know?

STEVE: I've had a few in my day.

Pause.

CHANG HYUN: You been wis Korean woman?

STEVE: Fuck, yeah, during the war. A bit shy at first, but once they get going they're fucking tigresses.

Silence.

CHANG HYUN: *(More hostility.)* You…take adbantage-uh…obu our woman.

Pause.

STEVE: War's hell. Nobody's perfect. You take it where you can get it.

Lights down—1-count.

Lights back up again.

CHANG HYUN and STEVE are laughing again and are even drunker.

STEVE sings "Doraji."

Doraji, doraji, bek doraji
Shimshin san chuneh bek doraji

Ju…Tyrone…taught me that one. Not bad for a Yank, huh?

STEVE: Let me teach you a game we play in these parts. It's called "Truth or Dare."

CHANG HYUN: Truce or dare.

STEVE: So you ask me, "Truth or dare?" If I pick truth, you ask me a question, any question at all. If I pick dare, you dare me to do something, something totally fucked-up and crazy. OK?

CHANG HYUN: OK.

STEVE: So, ask me: truth or dare?

CHANG HYUN: Truce or dare?

STEVE: Truth.

CHANG HYUN: OK, let's see…OK, I hab question.

Ip you hab only one day to lib, what you do?

Pause.

STEVE: *(Steely.)* Fuck.

CHANG HYUN: Puck?

STEVE: Guys.

CHANG HYUN: Oh.

Pause.

(Processing.) You…homosexual?

STEVE: I've told you all I know. I fuck guys and I love it.

Pause.

OK. Your turn. Truth or dare?

CHANG HYUN: Dare.

STEVE: Alright then.

Beat.

Come home with me.

Beat.

CHANG HYUN: What?

STEVE: Come home with me. I live just around the corner.

Pause.

CHANG HYUN: I don't sink so. I'm bery drunk.

STEVE: I've got soju at home.

Lights down—1-count.

Lights back up. STEVE's apartment.

CHANG HYUN takes his jacket off, slings it over the chair.

CHANG HYUN: *(Noticing the poster of Rocky Marciano.)* Rocky Marciano.

STEVE: You know him?

CHANG HYUN: Pamous boxer.

STEVE: What do you think of him?

CHANG HYUN: Neber see him pight.

STEVE: FYI, best boxer ever. 49 and 0. A perfect record.

Pause.

You like boxing?

CHANG HYUN: Yeah-yeah.

STEVE: Who's your favourite boxer?

CHANG HYUN: Byun Jong-il.

STEVE: Who?

CHANG HYUN: Korean boxer. World champion. Six year ago in Seoul Olympic he pight excellent pight, but judge decide against him, so he protest. Por one hour apter pight he sit in middle obu ring. He is my hero because he not apraid to stand up por himselp.

STEVE: I saw that fight. He deserved to lose.

CHANG HYUN: What?

STEVE: Jones walked all over him, but the fix was in. A few deals here and there and the gook got his gold. It was decided before it began. The most crooked thing I ever saw.

CHANG HYUN: *(Fuming.)* Korean deserbe to win! Por once Korea beat America and you don't like it. You hab to make up story to make Korea look bad. Because you always hab to win. You can't accept when you lose so you bring usser country down!

Silence.

STEVE seizes CHANG HYUN and tries to unzip his pants. CHANG HYUN resists. CHANG HYUN manages to push STEVE to the floor.

STEVE: *(Suddenly pathetic.)* Please…

Don't hate me… Please…

CHANG HYUN slowly moves to leave.

STEVE jumps up, grabs CHANG HYUN from behind and pins his hands behind his back.

(Pleadingly.) Please…

Let me have my way with you, just tonight… please…I promise I won't hurt you…please…just tonight…please.

He pushes CHANG HYUN against the wall and starts unzipping his pants from behind. CHANG HYUN pushes him away violently.

Silence.

OK, then, fuck me. I'll let you have your way with me. Come on.

He takes his pants off. CHANG HYUN runs to leave but STEVE grabs the gun from his pants, blocks CHANG HYUN's way, and points the gun at him.

(Matter-of-fact, without hostility.) Did you forget about this?

Get back in there. Easy does it. That's it. Good.

STEVE leads him back into the apartment, pushing him down on the floor.

CHANG HYUN is kneeling on the floor.

Alright, I'll make this easy for you. You don't have to fuck me. You don't even have to look at me. Just tell me how you fuck your girlfriend. Go on. From the beginning. Tell me how you ease it into her.

CHANG HYUN is still silent.

STEVE pushes the gun into the side of CHANG HYUN's head.

Practice your English. Start talking.

CHANG HYUN: Slowly…at pirst…slowly…gently…

STEVE: Yeah.

He puts his other hand inside his boxers.

CHANG HYUN: Den…I go paster…and deeper…

STEVE: *(Masturbating.)* Yeah, that's it.

CHANG HYUN: Paster…deeper…paster…deeper…

As STEVE seems close to coming, CHANG HYUN turns around, grabs the gun from STEVE and shoots. A flag with the word "BANG!" pops out of the gun.

I knew it. Just a toy.

He rises.

You crazy.

CHANG HYUN exits. He leaves his jacket.

Lights down.

Scene Fifteen

Lights up on CHANG HYUN, seated, and JAMIE, standing. School.

JAMIE: Ch—

CHANG HYUN: Jamie.

Pause.

I work out today. I sink my bicep getting bigger. I do new exercise call static contraction. Bery good exercise. *(He flexes his bicep.)* Peel.

JAMIE feels it.

JAMIE: *(Dryly.)* I'm lactating.

Pause.

CHANG HYUN: Are you…homosexual?

Beat.

JAMIE: I don't believe that to be an appropriate question.

CHANG HYUN: You ask me weird question.

JAMIE: Because I can. I'm the teacher.

CHANG HYUN: Why can you and I can't?

JAMIE: Because those are the rules. Plain and simple.

CHANG HYUN: I don't like dese rule.

JAMIE: Don't be so angry. Rules mean nothing beyond themselves. Remember what I said: it's all just play.

CHANG HYUN: Ip dat's da case, let's change-uh rule.

Pause.

JAMIE: *(Begrudgingly.)* Alright, then, just this once, you can ask the questions.

CHANG HYUN: OK. Are you homosexual?

Pause.

JAMIE: There's no such thing as homosexual. There's no such thing as heterosexual. There's no such thing as fact. There's no such thing as truth. It's all just play. Stories and points of view. Everything is nothing that we turn into something for our advantage.

CHANG HYUN: You're wrong. Dere is truce. Real ding happen to people. People's lipe change-uh. Dere is truce and dere is…consequence.

JAMIE: What there are are random happenings on which we as humans impose meaning and narrative. In and of itself, nothing has meaning.

CHANG HYUN: God gib meaning.

JAMIE: But God may not exist.

CHANG HYUN: He does!

JAMIE: He may not though. What happens then?

CHANG HYUN: We gib meaning.

JAMIE: But we are only human.

CHANG HYUN: But human lipe has meaning! Dere is story in what happen to us! We change-uh and grow!

JAMIE: Meaning is an illusion. It all depends on point of view. There's no such thing as truth.

Silence.

CHANG HYUN: My grandmahduh was raped by American soldier. She gib bird to his child—my pahduh. My pahduh he is bud. He can ply high. Away prom dose…who want to hurt him.

My grandmahduh is also bud. She ply highest obu all. I am not bud. I cannot ply high. I do not hab strong enup (enough) wing. Ip your wing is strong you can…swallow…da trud, let it lipt you to da sky…da sun.

Pause.

JAMIE: Meaning is an illusion. It all depends on point of view. There's no such thing as truth. Boy of fourteen, a baby-slash-house sitter. One weekend, he baby-slash-house-sits next door. They have two kids. Son. Daughter. Son is out for most of the night so he babysits Daughter. They make paper dolls. He reads her *Ramona the Pest*. By ten o'clock she's in bed. Son is home shortly after. Two hours later the sitter's dick is in Son's mouth. His eyes, his hair, his body, he's twelve. "If you don't suck my cock I'll fucking blow your brains out." Soon the babysitter's in juvenile detention. The end. Or. Once upon a time there lived a perfectly reliable and moral babysitter. One weekend he babysits for the couple next door—a nice enough tandem, if a tad bourgeois and very uptight. Deux enfants have they, a sporty son and an adorable daughter. The daughter's all of nine but the son's a quarter of a dozen years older. By ten o'clock the son's home from a night of Kool-aid and gangbanging, or whatever it is boys do when they get together on Saturday nights. When the clock strikes twelve the son emerges from his boudoir. His penis is quite literally about to burst through his shorts. He wags it in front of the sitter, who's trying to read King Lear. He unzips the sitter's pants and starts working on his scrotum. When the sitter comes to his senses he's already burst and screamed "Eureka!" They suck each other all night, almost drown in a sea of ejaculate. They have what by most accounts would be called a mutually pleasurable time. A few days later the police are on the sitter's doorstep. For the next half annis he's in juvenile detention, a victim of his sanctimonious society. So. Which story is true?

Beat.

Neither. It all depends on your point of view.

Pause.

CHANG HYUN: How old are you?

JAMIE: Thirty.

CHANG HYUN: You are older dan me, but seem younger. You seem…so pure. I like.

They look at each other.

CHANG HYUN places his hand on JAMIE's knee.

Slowly, it moves up to JAMIE's thigh. Finally, it moves to JAMIE's crotch.

JAMIE is breathing heavily, looks at once uncomfortable and excited.

JAMIE: This is dangerous. This is dangerous.

Slowly, tentatively, he puts his hand on CHANG HYUN's knee.

Lights down.

Scene Sixteen

MUSIC: Billie Holiday singing "Lover Man."

Lights up on STEVE's apartment. He is at the table, inebriated, holding himself, cradling himself, rocking back and forth subtly. He is starting to nod off, but struggling to stay awake.

Sound FX: Knock on the door.

STEVE starts, rises, picks up toy gun and "opens the door."

Light up on CHANG HYUN.

The music decrescendos.

STEVE: You're back. What are you, a masochist?

CHANG HYUN: *(Coldly.)* I porgot my jacket.

STEVE gets CHANG HYUN's jacket, which is slung over the chair. He hands it to CHANG HYUN.

STEVE: Anything else I can do for you?

CHANG HYUN: Why you carry dat toy?

STEVE snarls, laughs.

CHANG HYUN: Can I come in?

STEVE: *(Sarcastically, drunkenly.)* Can I come in. Can I come in. Forget it. This border's closed. Steve Wendland first. Now and forever.

CHANG HYUN pushes his way past STEVE.

Think you're tough, huh? You come here, foaming at the mouth with your self-righteous Commie bullshit, but it's all just words to you, fucking emissions from the mouth, in a language you don't even speak. Go ahead and practice your English. But I saw. *Saw.*

He pours himself another drink.

Sound FX: Gunshot.

STEVE reacts.

He starts mumbling to himself, as if in his own world.

The fucking death count. Ten degrees Fahrenheit, goddamn fucking freezing. Frozen palace of the dead. Their eyes still open. Beautiful, beautiful. They didn't fall asleep. Men till the very end. Ice men, ice kings. Twenty from our battalion. Eyes wide open. Lovely, lovely. Other guys breaking down. I vomit but go on. There to do a job. An arm, a torso, two legs, another arm. Our own Colonel Bartlett in five easy pieces, strapping bulk of man a pile of limbs on the side of the road.

STEVE starts singing softly.

Doraji, doraji, bek doraji
Shimshin san chuneh bek doraji

Ju…Tyrone…would sing that to me when I couldn't get to sleep. Some nights I couldn't coz I'd forget why we…

Sound FX: Gunshot.

STEVE reacts. Falters. Recovers.

Didn't matter that no one back home gave a damn.

Didn't matter that we didn't have a fucking clue what we were doing. My buddies, they…they died with their eyes open. Angels. All of 'em.

CHANG HYUN, who has been listening very intently, slowly moves behind STEVE.

Heroes, fucking heroes. They died…like men. Wish I went with 'em instead of/

CHANG HYUN pushes STEVE face down on the table. STEVE is too drunk to resist. He starts singing again.

Han dul pooriman kae-o-do
Dae guangjuri-e ch'ol ch'ol nomnunda

CHANG HYUN starts fucking STEVE, coldly, mechanically.

That's it. Sing it to me. Sing it till it kills me.

CHANG HYUN sings the song while fucking STEVE.

EUN HA moves downstage and now stands in front of STEVE.

STEVE sees her, vaguely extends an arm to her.

Lights fade out on CHANG HYUN and STEVE as the fucking accelerates and STEVE's moans crescendo. When the lights are out completely STEVE comes and gasps, but his gasp is less one of pleasure than of some indescribable pain.

Light change.

Korean countryside, 1953.

Sound FX: Sound of artillery barrage. Fade out.

50s RADIO REPORTER: *(V.O.)* U.S. troops and their allies have pushed

Communist forces back past the thirty-eighth parallel, a remarkable achievement considering that a mere three weeks ago all but ten percent of the Korean peninsula was in the hands of the enemy. But the fight is far from over. The goal is to rid all of Korea of the red menace, and to make the united peninsula a free and democratic society.

Light change.

EUN HA: *(To the audience.)* My brother, he told me that everything…is like water, do you understand? Loss becomes gain, what is ugly becomes beautiful. Everything…turns into its opposite.

A white doraji starts to bloom from the floor of the stage.

Kevin Kraussler (Jamie)

Act II

Darkness.

Billie Holiday is singing "In My Solitude."

A flame from a lighter in CHANG HYUN's apartment. JAMIE is smoking a joint.

The doraji continues to bloom from the floor of the stage.

Light out on JAMIE.

Light up on EUN HA and CHANG HYUN, Korea, 1994. They are hugging. CHANG HYUN is kneeling before EUN HA, whi is seated on a chair.

EUN HA slowly releases him.

CHANG HYUN: *(In Korean = perfect English.)* Grandmother, what am I going to do?

EUN HA: Be strong, Chang Hyun.

CHANG HYUN: I can't let you die.

EUN HA: Be strong. God will take care of you.

CHANG HYUN: He won't take care of me. He's never taken care of me. And now he's taking you away from me.

Pause.

EUN HA: God's ways are not our ways. We can't fight what we can't change. I've spent my whole life being angry. I'm ready to let go.

Light down on EUN HA.

Lights dim on CHANG HYUN, who transforms into TYRONE.

Lights up on TYRONE, Korea, 1950.

TYRONE is performing a traditional Korean folk dance in which he is imitating a crane. By turns he is waving his arms, whirling and bowing, and standing on one leg.

Lights up on STEVE approaching TYRONE.

He stands looking at STEVE for several seconds before TYRONE notices him.

STEVE slaps him hard on the face.

Pause.

TYRONE pulls out a white doraji from his pocket and gives it to STEVE.

STEVE throws it aside.

TYRONE runs off.

Lights down on STEVE.

Lights up on JAMIE, a joint in one hand, a Korean phrasebook in the other.

JAMIE: *(Reading from the phrasebook, slowly, deliberately, struggling with the pronunciation.)*

Annyong hashimnikka.

Chaemi ka ottosumnikka?

Ch'oum poepkessumnida.

Komapsupnida.

Put'akhamnida.

Ch'onmaneyo.

Annyongi chumushipshio.

Silence.

CHANG HYUN enters.

They look at each other.

JAMIE moves to kiss him. CHANG HYUN turns his face away.

CHANG HYUN turns JAMIE around, bends JAMIE over.

Lights down on CHANG HYUN and JAMIE.

Korea, early 50s.

Light on COLONEL BARTLETT (played by the actor who plays EUN HA).

COLONEL BARTLETT: *(To his soldiers.)* Boys, I know what you're going through. You'd hardly be the…decent, God-fearing boys you are…if you didn't feel what you're feeling. You have pity. You have heart. It's the faculty that's allows us to enjoy art, poetry, music. Puccini. *La Boheme.*

Singing from the aria "Mi Chiamans Mimi."

Ma quando vien lo sgelo,
Il primo sole e mio.
Il primo bacio del aprile e mio.
Il primo sole e mio.

These are exactly the things we are fighting for, the things that are sweet, that speak of love, of spring, that speak of dreams and of fancies, the things they call poetry. The freedom to enjoy them and to enjoy the aria Mimi sings about them—this is ultimately why we're here. Just keep that in mind every time you feel defeated by the sleepless nights, the hundred push-ups a morning, the crummy food, the gook pussies that have to substitute for the real thing.

Focus. Just focus. To focus…is the essence…of who we are. To narrow our vision, cut everything else out of our sight, cut a clear line from ourselves to the object and fire, just fire.

And remember that this…focus, this…tunnel-vision…obsessiveness…is what's brought about the great things of the world. From the pretty things, i.e. *La Boheme,* to the not-so-pretty, but necessary and good. And don't forget that, whatever horror, whatever…emptiness…you may feel, God is on our side. Never, ever forget that.

Light down on COLONEL BARTLETT.

Light up on CHANG HYUN and JAMIE, fucking.

CHANG HYUN comes.

JAMIE tries to kiss CHANG HYUN. CHANG HYUN turns his face away, exits.

Lights down on JAMIE.

Light up on EUN HA.

EUN HA: *(To the audience.)* Quiet night, not yet dawn. Father, father, he prayed that night, before dinner he did, he prayed for calm. Strange, I thought, how strange the prayer and…the way he said it, the angle of his voice. You're hiding something from me, I know it, you and Ju Cheol both, but I dare not say it. But my mother, my mother, she makes me forget. Beautiful mother, so placid her face, and her smile is soothing.

We knit durumagi, long, beautiful. While we knit we tell stories and we laugh, but I feel it. Father and

Ju Cheol are in the spare room arguing. Before bed I look out the window. The night sky is lovely. But a few hours later a symphony of northern artillery, shocking me out of sleep, rattling my body. Brown dust in early light. Chapter one.

Light down on EUN HA.

Lights up on STEVE's apartment. CHANG HYUN and STEVE are getting dressed, post-sex. STEVE starts coughing uncontrollably for several seconds.

CHANG HYUN: Are you OK?

STEVE: Yeah, why wouldn't I be?

STEVE's coughs subside.

Pause.

Say, you…you don't have to rush off. You're always rushing off.

CHANG HYUN: I hab to go. I must study por exam.

STEVE: Why…why don't you stay a bit? I got soju here. I bought it just for you.

CHANG HYUN sits down at the table.

STEVE pours him a drink. STEVE sits down.

Silence.

So, Windsor…my man.

Pause.

You're having a good time here in Vancouver?

CHANG HYUN nods.

Pause.

You're used to the rain now?

CHANG HYUN nods.

Pause.

You taking care of yourself?

CHANG HYUN nods.

Pause.

You go to the gym regularly?

CHANG HYUN nods.

Pause.

How much soju do I have to pump into you before you talk?

CHANG HYUN shrugs.

Silence.

What are you studying?

CHANG HYUN: Studying?

STEVE: In school.

CHANG HYUN: English.

STEVE: Besides that. You're taking other courses while you're here, right?

CHANG HYUN: Business administration.

STEVE: No kidding.

Beat.

A bit dry, isn't it?

CHANG HYUN: Pardon?

STEVE: You strike me as a…free spirit. I thought maybe you'd be in a different field.

CHANG HYUN: Like what?

STEVE: Oh, I don't know. Maybe…dance.

Silence.

Life's too short. Don't ever settle for something just because you feel you have to.

CHANG HYUN: I don't…settle. Whateber I hab to do I…lub.

STEVE: Just some advice from the wise and jaded. Take it or leave it.

Silence.

In dimmed lights we see JAMIE beginning to morph, with deliberate, ritualistic movements, into BRENDA.

So, uh…you get a lot of action back home?

CHANG HYUN: Pardon?

STEVE: I mean…what's it like being queer in Korea?

CHANG HYUN: Queer?

STEVE: Gay.

CHANG HYUN: I'm not gay.

Pause.

STEVE: Oops, I forgot. No fags in Korea. There. One thing you still haven't learned from America. The right to fuck whoever the fuck you want.

Pause.

How old are you?

CHANG HYUN: Twenty-two.

STEVE: You're younger than my son, I think.

CHANG HYUN: You hab son?

STEVE: *(Pouring himself a drink.)* So what if I do?

CHANG HYUN: But…you're gay.

STEVE: I knew you gooks were square about sex but this is ridiculous.

CHANG HYUN: So…you hab son.

STEVE: Yeah.

Light brightens on BRENDA.

BRENDA: *(To STEVE.)* Though you wouldn't recognize him if you saw him on the street, now, would you?

STEVE continues to speak as though oblivious to BRENDA.

STEVE: It's been awhile since I've seen him.

BRENDA: Twenty-eight years, six months and thirteen days.

STEVE: I wonder about him.

BRENDA: Please, all you ever cared about was booze and boys.

STEVE: He's a teacher, I think…or something like that.

BRENDA: Look…I knew you had a thing for guys when I married you. I figured, who am I to judge? Personally I like doing it with a swing and dessert toppings.

STEVE: He's older than you.

BRENDA: He just turned thirty, Colonel Wendland.

STEVE: His mother never let me see him.

BRENDA: That's right, Colonel, keep it clean. Once you

chickened out and crossed the forty-ninth parallel I never heard from you ever again.

CHANG HYUN: Do you…regret…dat you not see him?

BRENDA: *(To CHANG HYUN.)* Regret? You don't know Steve Wendland. This guy zooms through life like Mario Andretti at the Indy. *(To STEVE.)* One thing I'll hand you—you were fantastic in bed. Relentless, insatiable, like you could never have enough. When we fucked there was—there was always this wild thing about you, this look in your eyes like you were being chased or…you were chasing something. And you were always far away, never… really there, you know, like…like screwing me was just your way of getting somewhere else. But maybe that's why I was with you in the first place. The more unattainable someone is the more…in love with them you are.

She touches STEVE's face.

What were you chasing, Stevie? And what were you running from?

STEVE: You do what you have to do.

BRENDA: Bingo, baby. You do what you have to do. Which is why I don't blame you for running off to Canada. Korea fucked you up—why go to hell twice?

STEVE: So no. No regrets.

BRENDA: Really? None? You're a bitter, lonely, sex-addicted boozehound with nothing but war memories and a fatal disease. You've become your worst fear—an old queen wasting away. The lights are going out, Stevie—whatever you're chasing, hurry.

Lights down on BRENDA, CHANG HYUN and STEVE.

Light up on EUN HA.

EUN HA: *(To the audience.)* Six months in, the north had stormed through and destroyed everything. Miraculously, our village stayed in tact. Yes, what I knew remained as is, which you might think was a comfort but…I'd rather they'd destroyed everything right away, do you understand? I'd have done away with the illusion that everything would be fine. But six months pass before it happens, my biggest shame, I encouraged Ju Cheol to volunteer with the Americans.

Light up on the figure of JU CHEOL in his army clothes.

When he left my bones felt it, the ground beneath, the great shift.

In dimmed lights JAMIE places a gardenia behind his ear and becomes BILLIE HOLIDAY.

Light up on BILLIE singing "You Go To My Head," a capella.

Lights down on BILLIE.

The lighting of a cigarette.

Lights up on CHANG HYUN and JAMIE in CHANG HYUN's apartment.

They are in bed, CHANG HYUN fucking JAMIE from behind while smoking. They are clothed.

CHANG HYUN ejaculates.

Pause.

CHANG HYUN: Summer. Sunny. Lobely.

JAMIE gets out of bed. CHANG HYUN pours himself a drink, continues to smoke.

So. You hate Korea?

JAMIE: I told you—I blamed Koreans for the fact that I never had a father. I agree, it's ironic that I've ended up fucking one.

Pause.

By the way, Kim Il-sung died today.

CHANG HYUN: How you know?

JAMIE: It was on the radio. It was the lead story in the news.

Pause.

This could very well be a watershed moment. The man was a maniac, a tyrant, a demagogue, depriving his people of their inherent right to look outwards. Now that he's gone and with the collapse of Communism everywhere, the two Koreas may soon go the way of the two Germanys. There's something happening in the world, don't you think? A new—enlightenment? A universal—understanding?

Pause.

CHANG HYUN: *(Angry.)* I should stop call you Jamie and start call you Maria bon Trapp, uh—Unibersal understanding? Why not understand Korea? Nors Korean are crazy, but dere is reason dey're crazy. And unibersal understanding cannot pix dat. You don't know what you're talking about.

JAMIE: I didn't know it was a crime to be an idealist.

CHANG HYUN: So innocent. So naï-buh.

JAMIE: Naï*ve*.

CHANG HYUN: Naï-buh!

CHANG HYUN turnsaway from JAMIE.

Light change.

Lights up on EUN HA, seated as in the Prelude, except that this time she is facing CHANG HYUN.

EUN HA: *(In Korean = perfect English.)* They hurt you in the military, didn't they?

CHANG HYUN kneels down before her, bows his head.

She puts her arms around him. He cries quietly. 10 count.

They speak in Korean = perfect English.

EUN HA: Now I know why you've been acting the way you have since you've come back.

CHANG HYUN: I didn't want to tell you. I didn't want you to know. I was hoping you would…die…before you found out…

Silence.

EUN HA: The core has exploded. The ground's been pulled from under you.

It's a haze, isn't it. You don't know where you are. Look at me.

CHANG HYUN slowly looks up at her.

Stand up.

He stands up.

Touch your hair.

They both touch their hair.

Your face.

Their both touch their face.

Your arms.

They both touch their arms.

Your legs.

They both touch their legs.

There now.

She stands up, holds his face in her hands.

You are here.

Pause.

CHANG HYUN: Halmeoni, I feel as though…I'm worth nothing.

EUN HA: You are worth nothing. You're just a pack of cells following the laws of nature. You're just a body in the military defending an artificial border. To the world outside, you're a tool. You must fly inside to find the sun.

She grabs his body.

Because you belong…to you.

Light down on EUN HA.

Light bright again on JAMIE.

CHANG HYUN and JAMIE look at each other.

CHANG HYUN slowly takes his socks off.

JAMIE slowly takes off his.

CHANG HYUN slowly takes his shirt off.

JAMIE slowly takes off his.

CHANG HYUN slowly takes his pants off.

JAMIE slowly takes off his.

CHANG HYUN slowly takes his briefs off.

JAMIE slowly takes off his.

The doraji blooms some more.

CHANG HYUN and JAMIE move closer to each other.

JAMIE turns his head away from CHANG HYUN.

CHANG HYUN takes JAMIE's face and forces JAMIE to look at him.

JAMIE once again turns his head away from CHANG HYUN.

CHANG HYUN once again takes JAMIE's face and forces JAMIE to look at him.

The doraji blooms some more.

CHANG HYUN starts touching JAMIE's hair.

He takes JAMIE's hand and puts it on his own hair. JAMIE starts touching CHANG HYUN's hair.

CHANG HYUN starts touching JAMIE's face.

JAMIE starts touching CHANG HYUN's face.

CHANG HYUN starts touching JAMIE's hands.

JAMIE starts touching CHANG HYUN's hands.

Their bodies move closer to each other as they continue to touch each other, the touching becoming more sensuous.

CHANG HYUN slaps JAMIE hard on the face.

JAMIE slaps CHANG HYUN hard on the face.

CHANG HYUN starts kissing JAMIE, slowly, hesitantly at first, then passionately.

The doraji blooms some more.

Lights down on CHANG HYUN and JAMIE.

Lights up on EUN HA.

EUN HA: *(Still in previous conversation with CHANG HYUN.)* There. All quiet now. Nothing looking over you. You are free.

Lights up on CHANG HYUN and JAMIE.

JAMIE goes inside CHANG HYUN.

They fuck.

They both come.

They lie together.

The doraji blooms some more.

They speak tenderly.

JAMIE: *(Perfectly.)* Chamulsoe.

Naengsu.

Mogijang.

Ach'im siksa.

CHANG HYUN: *(Perfectly.)* Food.

Perfect.

Vilify.

Feather.

Pause.

JAMIE: First day of autumn. Beautiful.

CHANG HYUN rises, puts his clothes on, and starts singing "Edelweiss."

Lights change as CHANG HYUN morphs into TYRONE while singing "Doraji."

TYRONE: Doraji, doraji, bek doraji
Shimshin / san chuneh bek doraji /
Han dul pooriman / kae-o-do
Dae guangjuri-e ch'ol / ch'ol nomnunda

Lights up on TYRONE. He is crouching with pencil and pad, drawing.

Lights up on STEVE.

He goes to TYRONE, snatches pad from him.

He looks at it.

He throws it aside.

He starts to beat TYRONE.

STEVE: *(While he's beating TYRONE.)* Sketch this, you son of a bitch!

TYRONE:

	English translation.
Weh geu rae yo?	Why are you doing this?

STEVE: Sketch blood, guts, corpses frozen in / the ice.

TYRONE:

	English translation.
Kuman!!	No more!

STEVE: Sketch my buddies fucking hanging themselves, sketch me going into a fucking / loony bin!

TYRONE:

	English translation.
Chebal, kuman haeyo! Ap'ayo!	Stop it! Please! You're hurting me!

STEVE stops beating TYRONE.

STEVE wraps his head in his arms, collapses on the floor. He is rocking back and forth.

Silence.

TYRONE slowly rises and advances towards STEVE.

TYRONE: *(Gently, in Korean = perfect English.)* No one told you how deep the sea is.

TYRONE pulls out a doraji from his pocket and offers it to STEVE.

STEVE looks at it for a moment, then takes it.

Lights down on STEVE and TYRONE.

The doraji from the floor of the stage blooms some more.

Lights up on STEVE, CHANG HYUN and JAMIE in their respective apartments. They are addressing the audience.

JAMIE: And so my books, the only things that have kept me going all these years, they've…they've made of my mind a weapon, in the world I have not been small.

STEVE: I want to sit, do you understand? I've been running all my life. I just…want to sit, but…I've run out of chairs.

CHANG HYUN: *(In Korean = perfect English.)* Everything…was so clear…sunlight everywhere, all the time, everyone speaking in one voice, I…I never had to think.

JAMIE: But now I've no size he—he's made me small again. As I open, and open, the force of the world pushes me down.

STEVE: So Windsor he comes over all right, and…and we

do what we do and it's done and then it's, how do I explain it, like he's cradling himself or something, holding himself from the world or, or…teetering on the brink of something, keeping himself from falling.

CHANG HYUN: *(In Korean = perfect English.)* But now it's all… dark…they both…obscure the sun, they…are pools from which I drink and into which I fall.

JAMIE: I am tiny again and helpless, want to close down, re—regain size, but somehow I keep opening, what I am embracing I cannot hold.

STEVE: And I want to talk to him, you know? Not at but, but...I want to see him through it.

CHANG HYUN: *(In Korean = perfect English.)* I don't know myself anymore, everything's…upside down. Their pools…poison…and I can no longer…see.

Lights down on JAMIE, STEVE and CHANG HYUN.

Lights up on EUN HA.

EUN HA: *(To the audience.)* From there more shifts, the strands loosening, tearing apart the fabric. The village nearby became a heap of wood and bones, we went south to live with uncle, ants scurrying to another cleft. In two weeks my father, body shriveled to a sliver, shitting and vomiting blood, skin…blanched and—and rashed, hands toward me like I am God, beseeching, hanging on. But I am not God, when I'm alone I am screaming. With my father's last breath, I saw God's true colours.

Light up on JAMIE, seated, in school. Across from him is an empty chair. He glances at his watch, looks desolate.

Light down on JAMIE as CHANG HYUN

approaches MAN #3 (played by the actor playing EUN HA. CHANG HYUN kneels down, starts giving MAN #3 a blow job.

Light down on CHANG HYUN and MAN #3.

Light up on STEVE in his apartment, inebriated. Just as he's about to take another sip of his drink he starts coughing uncontrollably. He rises, walks slowly around the room, banging his hands on the walls, the table, the chair, in an effort to stop the coughing.

Light down on STEVE and light up on JAMIE in his apartment, pacing frantically back and forth. He picks up the phone and dials.

Sound FX: Phone rings three times.

GENERIC VOICE ON ANSWERING MACHINE: Please leave a message after the tone.

JAMIE hurls the phone on the floor.

Light down on JAMIE and light up on MAN #3 fucking CHANG HYUN.

Light down on CHANG HYUN and MAN #3 and light up on STEVE vomiting.

Light down on STEVE.

Light up on JAMIE in his apartment, holding himself, cradling himself, rocking back and forth subtly.

Light up on CHANG HYUN in his apartment, kneeling by his bed, praying.

Light up on STEVE vomiting.

Lights down on JAMIE, STEVE and CHANG HYUN.

Lights up on EUN HA.

EUN HA: *(To the audience.)* All the pain of the world, the weight of it all. *(Reacts as though to a memory of kick inside her belly.)* Our fear, our hatred, our disgust, our madness, planted and growing in my body. *(Reacts as though to a memory of a kick inside her belly.)*

Lights down on EUN HA.

Korea, early 50s.

Lights up on STEVE and TYRONE in the barracks.

It is night. TYRONE is sleeping.

STEVE is holding himself, cradling himself, rocking back and forth subtly.

TYRONE awakes, sees STEVE.

He holds STEVE by the shoulders, stops his rocking.

TYRONE:	*(Tenderly.)*	*English translation.*
	Nae ryuh wa.	Fall.
	Kunyan, nae ryuh wa.	Just fall.

With his hands he makes a gesture that indicates "fall."

Light down on STEVE, light dims on TYRONE.

In dimmed lights CHANG HYUN/TYRONE places a gardenia behind his ear and becomes BILLIE HOLIDAY.

Lights up on BILLIE with her white gardenia,

singing "What A Little Moonlight Can Do," a capella.

On her last few lines the lights fades out on her, and we hear male voices muttering in the dark.

Korea, 1994.

Darkness. The voices continue after BILLIE finishes singing.

VOICES: *(One at a time, not together.)* You think your shit doesn't stink?

You think you're better than everyone else?

	English translation.
Niga taedanhan jul anya?	Think you're so tough?
Yee mat jjom pabua.	See if you can take this.

The sound of bodies struggling against each other, then CHANG HYUN gasping and then screaming. The sound of thrusting and screaming continues for 10 seconds. We hear some laughing, finally the sound of men running away.

Moonlight on CHANG HYUN sprawled face down on the floor, his body facing upstage, arms and legs spread out, briefs pulled down to his knees.

CHANG HYUN rises, his back to the audience, pulls his briefs up.

Lights up on STEVE in his apartment, hunched over the table.

CHANG HYUN goes to STEVE, fucks him very angrily in slow, deliberate rhythms.

CHANG HYUN: *(While he's fucking STEVE, in Korean = perfect English.):*

You think you're better than everyone else.

	English translation.
Niga taedanhan jul anya?	Think you're so tough?
Yee mat jjom pabua.	See if you can take this.

They both come after about ten thrusts.

CHANG HYUN pulls out of STEVE.

They rise from the table.

CHANG HYUN starts putting his clothes on.

STEVE: Why are you always in such a rush?

CHANG HYUN: I told you, I'm busy.

STEVE: At the risk of sounding like a woman, you make me feel cheap.

Pause.

Hey, I bought you something.

He pulls out a bouquet of white bellflowers from under the table.

I thought it might, you know, remind you of home.

CHANG HYUN: I don't really like white doraji. I preper blue.

STEVE: Oh. Well, take it anyway. And stay a bit, won't you? It's cold in here, you know, and, and…not happy.

CHANG HYUN: I don't come here to make you happy.

STEVE: You're using me and that's fine, but maybe, just sometimes you can…pretend.

CHANG HYUN: What you want prom me?

Sound FX: Gunshot.

STEVE reacts.

Pause.

STEVE: You know, Ju…Tyrone, he pointed something out about me. He told me that sometimes I hold myself like…I'm on the brink of something, you know? Like I'm…keeping myself from falling.

You do the same thing, you know? So I'll give you the advice he gave me:

Fall. Just fall.

Forget everything you were ever told and just…fall.

Silence.

CHANG HYUN: I won't pall. I can't pall.

Angry.

You can't make me / pall!

STEVE: Hey, re / lax.

CHANG HYUN: I don't want your adbice…

I don't want anysing prom you…

I don't…know why…I'm here…

As he frantically finishes getting dressed. To himself.

	English translation.
Todeh chech nega, ottoke yogi kaji oun gawji?	Why am I here? Why am I doing…what I'm doing?
Na…to isang irokke mot salgesso…na…ppajiji ankesso.	I can't do this anymore…I will not…fall.

STEVE: You've been on a power trip from fucking me and now that I ask for kindness you can't handle it.

Guess I had it coming. What goes around comes around.

		English translation.
CHANG HYUN:	Na irokke mot salgesso…	I can't do this anymore…
	Na…ku saram ttaemune sangcho an padulle…	I—I can't let them …hurt me…

STEVE: No one forced you to do anything you didn't want to do, so don't start playing victim boy just coz you want out.

CHANG HYUN: *(Out of himself now, pointing at STEVE.)*: You…you American…

You hurt us so much…already…

You…will not change-uh me…

I…will not pall…

Sound FX: Gunshot.

STEVE reacts.

Pause.

STEVE: You got what you wanted, didn't you?

We're even.

Pause.

CHANG HYUN turns to leave.

STEVE stops him, hands him the flowers.

CHANG HYUN looks at the flowers. Tableau. Lights dim on CHANG HYUN and STEVE.

Light on EUN HA.

Sound FX: A baby crying.

EUN HA covers her ears.

VOICE #1: It shows.

VOICE #2: His hair's light-coloured.

VOICE #3: He's a child of the devil.

VOICE #1: You're abhorrent.

VOICE #2: You're shameful.

VOICE #3: You're a slut.

Light dims on EUN HA.

Light brightens on STEVE and CHANG HYUN.

CHANG HYUN takes the flowers and throws them on the floor.

CHANG HYUN: You look tired.

Go to sleep.

He exits.

Lights dim on STEVE who places a gardenia behind his hair and becomes BILLIE HOLIDAY.

Screen: Images of the Korean War.

50s RADIO REPORTER: *(V.O.)* U.S. troops have crushed Communist forces in Chunchun, just south of the Thirty-Eighth parallel. Chinese and North Korean forces have launched a vicious offensive, but our boys countered magnificently. During the last three weeks, over sixty-five thousand enemy troops have been killed, fostering hope that the Korean peninsula may yet, God willing, be free of the red menace.

Light on BILLIE. BILLIE sings "Good Morning, Heartache," a capella.

Lights down on BILLIE.

Lights up. JAMIE and CHANG HYUN in school, seated in their usual chairs.

JAMIE: Chang Hyun. Surprised to see you back.

Pause.

You've been absent for three whole weeks.

Pause.

For this entire scene CHANG HYUN speaks in Korean = perfect English.

CHANG HYUN: I have no intention of wasting my father's money.

JAMIE: English only.

CHANG HYUN shakes his head.

English. Only.

Silence.

So. First topic.

Pause.

Why haven't you returned my calls? Why have you been avoiding me?

Pause.

CHANG HYUN: Because you're sick.

Disgusting.

You're immoral, a pervert, an abomination.

You can't bring me down. You won't.

I am not like you. I will never be like you.

You and your country have raped me.

But I'm free of you now. I'm free.

Silence.

JAMIE: I hear you're going back to Korea next week.

He stands up, offers his hand.

It was a pleasure teaching you. Goodbye.

CHANG HYUN looks at JAMIE's hand. He refuses it and instead bows his head.

He exits.

JAMIE sits down. Lights down.

Lights up on EUN HA.

EUN HA: *(To the audience.)* My baby, my baby. How I hated him at first, but what is loss becomes gain, what is ugly becomes beautiful. Everything…is like water. The whole of everything in my child. The whole… of everything…in you…and in me.

Light on EUN HA dims.

Lights up on STEVE and JAMIE in their respective apartments, phones in hand. STEVE is in bed, JAMIE is seated on the floor.

The following exchange to be performed slowly, hesitantly.

STEVE: Hi.

JAMIE: Yeah, hi.

Pause.

STEVE: What do you look like?

JAMIE: Five-ten, one sixty, brown hair, blue eyes.

STEVE: Nice. *(Beat.)* How old are you?

JAMIE: Thirty. *(Beat.)* How old are you?

STEVE: Doesn't matter.

Pause.

You OK?

JAMIE: Yeah.

STEVE: You sound nervous.

JAMIE: Not nervous, just excited.

Pause.

(Desperately.) Give it to me yeah stick it in me your long thick cock yeah pump your joy juice into me yeah that's it/fuck me.

STEVE: Ssssh, slow down. Just get out of a monastery?

Silence.

Hey.

What's wrong?

Pause.

(Tenderly.) Easy now.

Easy does it.

That's it.

Ssssh.

Silence.

They are not masturbating.

There.

Pause.

You're strong now.

Keep your chin up.

You're beautiful.

The doraji blooms some more.

Lights down on JAMIE and STEVE.

Light on EUN HA brightens.

EUN HA: *(To the audience.)* With borders, six billion whirlpools.

Without, the world is one lake.

The burden is shared, your pain is mine.

You begin to merge with the air.

Light on EUN HA dims.

Light up on JAMIE, smoking a joint.

Sound FX: Phone ringing. After 3 rings it goes to answering machine.

VOICE ON ANSWERING MACHINE: Please leave a message after the tone.

VOICE OF CHANG HYUN: Hello, Jamie. Dis is…Windsor. Chang Hyun.

I…go back to Seoul next week.

I'm…sorry dat I not see you por so long bepore today, but…I habuh bery muchee on my mind. Many soughts (thoughts). Bery hard.

Light on CHANG HYUN, phone in hand. He is speaking in tandem with his voiceover. Eventually the voiceover fades out.

I habuh to go home. My parent need me.

I…guess…I not see you again.

Sank you…por teaching me. I learn muchee.

You…are bery good…and bery kind.

Um…I…I know…you like reading. Dere is Korean poem dat remind me obu you.

"Amudo geuge susimeul illeojun ili eobsgie heuinnabineun domuji badaga museobji anhda"

English translation.

"Since no one has ever told you how deep the sea is the whte butterfly has no fear of the sea."

It is dippicult to translate, but it is about white butterply.

You are like…white butterply.

I like.

CHANG HYUN hangs up. Lights out on him.

EUN HA looks at JAMIE. Extends an arm.

The doraji blooms some more.

Slowly, lights go down on JAMIE and EUN HA.

Phantasmagoric sound FX.

MUSIC: Billie Holiday singing "I'm A Fool To Want You."

On top of this, the voice of a 50s RADIO BOXING COMMENTATOR comes in.

50s RADIO BOXING COMMENTATOR: And Marciano's really turning it up now. Huge left from Marciano. And another one! No one can put as much weight into a punch as Marciano.

Lights up on STEVE in his apartment, seated, inebriated, looking very frail, struggling to stay awake. He is holding himself, cradling himself, rocking back and forth subtly.

MUSIC: Morphs from jazz to the army tune.

MALE VOICES: Fly the Stars and Stripes high
For freedom and peace are nigh
Shout for victory and make a pledge that men will be free.
Brothers forever
Place your trust in me
Fly the Stars and Stripes high
For peace and freedom are nigh

50s RADIO REPORTER: *(V.O., overlapping slightly with the MALE VOICES.)* Our boys are trudging bravely on, despite the fact that the enemy, even with inferior weaponry, is proving a more formidable opponent than expected. But evil is formidable—no one should ever pretend otherwise. And we must never allow lack of success to devalue the worth of righteous action.

Sounds of war continue as lights go down.

Sounds of war fade away.

Light on TYRONE, serving as a night guard.

STEVE: *(Remembering, hallucinating, seeing TYRONE.)* Ju Cheol! Don't fall asleep! That'll be the death of us!

A CHINESE SOLDIER enters behind TYRONE and shoots him in the back. TYRONE falls to the ground.

Light up on EUN HA, approaching TYRONE.

EUN HA: *(Taking TYRONE in her arms)* Anything…everything turns into its opposite. The closing of the door, instant, not gradual. Loss of all hope, no turning back.

Light up on STEVE. He is speaking to the audience.

STEVE: After that, made…made amends, became the best soldier in the battalion. Wasn't a command I wasn't on top of, that I didn't relish…carrying out.

Kill'em… kill'em all…

Just…following orders…

So I did it…just did it…every gook I saw on the battlefield. Man, woman, child…couldn't risk missing a Commie.

As he says this, SHADOW of YOUNG STEVE in Korea, approaching the SHADOW of an OLD WOMAN caught in the battlefield. He guns her down.

Remorse? Not really. Had it coming, the whole country did, they got us into this mess so every one of them deserved to die.

SHADOWS disappear.

EUN HA: No more tears I can muster, the night was never darker but the peak had been climbed. Killed by the very ones who we thought were our saviours. All feeling spent, my heart like stone. All's shifted, subverted, what made me laugh now made me vomit.

SHADOWS of YOUNG STEVE and a NORTH KOREAN SOLDIER in a war prison. The NORTH KOREAN SOLDIER is beating STEVE senseless.

STEVE: Eventually they, they got me. Beat me…starved me...

The NORTH KOREAN SOLDIER starts raping STEVE.

(As THE SHADOWS disappear.) Got…got so thin after six months, slipped under the barbed wire and escaped. Yeah, I was recaptured but for two weeks I was…free. Fourteen whole days. Felt like a hero, a winner.

SHADOW of YOUNG STEVE, dancing around in a half-celebratory, half-crazed manner.

Delirious, fucking…delirious, head spinning… spinning with pride…I was so full of life, wanted to share it with the whole world. Unbeatable, untouchable, my insides bursting…to fill the universe.

Pause.

SHADOW of YOUNG STEVE is still.

This girl…this farm girl…

Electric in the sunlight…

I was bursting…bursting…

I just needed her to catch me...

The SHADOW disappears.

EUN HA: I could not exist, but he existed fully.

His past, his present. His want, his need. His strength, his weakness. His body, his world.

His story in his act, while I was nothing.

Later, only later did I feel the weight of his body,

crushing me…crushing me as he himself was being crushed.

The weight so much heavier than one body, one man.

A body, a world. Shame on us all.

The light on EUN HA is exceedingly bright.

Lights down on EUN HA and STEVE.

Blood oozes out of the doraji.

Lights up on STEVE in his apartment, in bed.

SOUND FX: Knock on the door.

STEVE: It's open.

CHANG HYUN enters.

(He is sober.) I'm not feeling well enough to get up. Sorry. Your jacket's on the chair. Put it on before you forget it again.

CHANG HYUN puts his jacket on.

Good. Thanks for coming. Didn't think you would.

CHANG HYUN: I wasn't going to but/I

STEVE: *(Smiling.)* You can't resist me. *(He starts coughing. The coughing lasts for many seconds.)*

CHANG HYUN: *(Over the coughing.)* Are you OK?

He goes to STEVE, pours him a glass of water, assists him as he drinks it.

STEVE: Thank you.

Beat.

CHANG HYUN: Why you want to see me?

STEVE: Just to say thank you.

The doraji blooms some more.

CHANG HYUN: *(Sitting down on the chair next to the bed.)* You don't look well.

STEVE: I'm not. I'm dying.

Beat.

It's neither here nor there so please don't ask any questions.

Pause.

STEVE reaches under the pillow beside him, reveals his toy gun. He hands it to CHANG HYUN.

Here. Keep it.

A souvenir.

CHANG HYUN takes it.

He points it towards the side of his head, pulls the trigger. The flag with the word "pow" pops out.

Pause.

Kiss me.

CHANG HYUN: What?

STEVE: Just kiss me.

CHANG HYUN: I don't sink I / want to.

STEVE: We've been fucking for six months and we've never once kissed.

STEVE pulls CHANG HYUN's head to him and kisses him on the lips, tenderly.

The doraji blooms some more.

When are you going back to Korea?

CHANG HYUN: Tomorrow.

STEVE: Got your suitcases packed?

CHANG HYUN nods.

Pause.

I'm sorry.

CHANG HYUN: Por what?

STEVE: Read into it whatever you want. I'm not saying it again.

Pause.

STEVE starts coughing again. The coughs subside a bit more quickly this time.

I told you how many times I almost died in Korea, didn't I?

CHANG HYUN nods.

I love your country. It's a part of me.

Pause.

What's your name?

CHANG HYUN: You know my name.

STEVE: Your real name.

CHANG HYUN: Chang Hyun.

Pause.

STEVE: What are you gonna do when you go home?

CHANG HYUN: Pinish school, work por my pahduh, get married.

Silence.

I…don't know…

Silence.

CHANG HYUN holds himself, cradles himself. He is rocking back and forth subtly.

STEVE grabs CHANG HYUN by the shoulders, stops his rocking, whispers something in his ear.

CHANG HYUN nods. Smiles.

Pause.

STEVE: Thank you.

Beat.

CHANG HYUN: You already sank me.

Pause.

STEVE: *(Mumbling to himself.)* If this were Korea forty-five years ago this scene would be a hell of a lot nobler.

Pause.

Stand up.

Just stand up.

CHANG HYUN stands up.

Turn around.

CHANG HYUN turns around.

Now start walking. Slowly.

CHANG HYUN starts walking slowly.

Now sing it.

Pause.

C'mon, start singing.

CHANG HYUN: *(Walking away, visibly puzzled.)* Doraji, doraji, bek doraji
Shimshin / san chuneh bek doraji

STEVE: Keep walking and don't look back. Lock the door on your way out.

CHANG HYUN: Han dul pooriman kae-o-do
Dae guangjuri-e ch'ol ch'ol nomnunda

CHANG HYUN is now out of sight.

Sound FX: Door locking from the inside and closing.

No sound or action for five seconds while STEVE waits.

Slowly, with a struggle, he sits himself up.

From under his pillow he produces a revolver. He looks at it.

Light up on EUN HA.

She crosses to STEVE.

EUN HA looks at him intently and coldly.

Gradually, her look becomes gentler, even compassionate. She sits next to him on the bed.

He is holding himself, cradling himself, rocking back and forth subtly.

EUN HA grabs him by the shoulders, stops his rocking.

		English translation.
EUN HA:	Nae ryuh na.	Fall.

Kunyan, nae ryuh na. Just fall.

She makes a gesture with her hands that indicates "fall."

STEVE nods, smiles.

He sticks the barrel into his mouth. He begins to shake.

EUN HA holds his other hand.

Light change.

50s RADIO BOXING COMMENTATOR: *(V.O.)* Marciano's keeping the pressure…superb right hook by Marciano…and another one...and Moore's down!

AUDIENCE: *(V.O., chanting in the background):* One…two… three…four…five…six…seven…eight…

50s RADIO BOXING COMMENTATOR: *(V.O.)* And it's over! Marciano has retained the world title! Make that forty-nine straight wins for the Brockton Bomber, perhaps the greatest boxer the world has ever known!

AUDIENCE: *(V.O., chanting.)* Rocky, Rocky, Rocky, Rocky, Rocky, Rocky, Rocky, Rocky, Rocky, etc.

Light changes back as chanting fades out.

Shaking, STEVE pulls the trigger.

At the sound of the gun the lights snap out on STEVE and EUN HA.

The doraji blooms some more.

Lights up on JAMIE, centre stage.

JAMIE: His body, his world. Inside me forever.

The rivers, the flowers, the hailstorms, the graves.

Hand grenades at dawn. Caresses at twilight.

Every colour under the sun in his world, my heart.

To open is to surrender to the sea and to the sky.

And to grow is to receive both the rain and the light.

The doraji continues to bloom until finally it covers the entire stage, vertically and horizontally. It glows fiercely in the dark.

The End.